THE MAGIC

OF

SELLING

I, your wizard, *per ardua ad alta*,
am about to embark on a hazardous
and technically unexplainable journey
into the outer stratosphere!
To confer, converse, and otherwise
hobnob with my brother wizards.

—Wizard of Oz (Frank Morgan)
The Wizard of Oz (1939)

To believe in yourself.
To know why you sell.
To be untouchable.
That's the magic of selling.

I don't believe in the kind of magic in my books. But I do believe something very magical can happen when you read a good book.

–J. K. Rowling

THE MAGIC

OF

SELLING

ROBERT MILLER

Printed in the United States of America

ISBN 978-0-9975887-0-5

To Mom

selling

the process of persuading others to buy a product or service or accept, approve, or adopt a concept or cause

You are about to discover the magic of selling. Rod Serling, the creator of the *Twilight Zone*, said: "If in any quest for magic, in any search for sorcery, witchery, legerdemain, first check the human spirit." This book will take you on a **Magical Mystery Tour** as you remember some of the songs and stories you have heard or read. My message is not about magic, but about the human spirit. Finally, the key to magic is always the human spirit. And the purest magic is within us.

You'll follow the Yellow Brick Road and travel to the Land of Oz with Dorothy, Toto, the Tin Woodman, the Scarecrow, and the Cowardly Lion. You'll meet the Wizard of Oz and discover that the magic of the Emerald City is nothing more than make-believe and the not so wonderful wizard is not so magical after all.

You and Alice will go through the looking glass to Wonderland, a fantastic place full of bizarre adventures, and meet the Mad Hatter, Caterpillar, Cheshire Cat, White Rabbit, and other magical characters. Peter Pan will fly with you to Neverland, an imaginary faraway place where Tinker Bell, the Lost Boys, and mythical creatures and beings live.

Mickey Mouse will share with you his magical experience as the Sorcerer's Apprentice in Fantasia.

Your heart will go pit-a-pat as you get in a fix after fix with Felix the Cat (the wonderful, wonderful cat) and his magical little bag of tricks.

Magic is all around us. Maybe not the kind they teach at the Hogwarts School of Witchcraft and Wizardry; but the kind you know exists in your heart and mind and the hearts and minds of others.

By the time you finish *The Magic of Selling* you will be a wizard if you believe in yourself and believe that *you create your own magic*. Selling is a virtual Ouija Board. By discovering why you sell and why people buy you will understand the power of four magical words: "Like me. Buy Now.

Abracadabra!

Robert Miller

Contents

The only thing you've got in this world
is what you can sell.

—Arthur Miller
Death of a Salesman (1949)

Selling

We didn't sell women an exercise machine. We sold them a dream and showed them how to make it come true. That was the "magic" of the Stauffer Magic Couch.

–Marion Miller
Beverly Hills, California
(Sometime in the Fabulous Fifties)

SELLING

Before I was born, my mother was a fashion model. After having three kids, she still looked like a fashion model. In the early 1950's she met B.H. Stauffer, inventor of "The Stauffer System." He claimed that his system could help America's housewives get a slender, youthful-looking figure by just passively laying on his "magic couch" after stating that exercise was vital to good health and a "lovely shape". Stauffer contended that his Magic Couch would do the work for you while you relaxed, read, napped, watched TV, or talked on the telephone. Following remarkable success in weight reduction salons across America, Stauffer introduced the Stauffer Home Reducing Plan which included the Posture-Rest. It was a portable, lightweight machine which could be rented or purchased.

America was at the beginning of an obsession with weight loss. Post-war prosperity had packed on "extra pounds" on some people who would do whatever they could to be slender. Given a choice between a workout at a Vic Tanny Center or laying on the Magic Couch and watching the *Betty Crocker Star Matinee*, many people opted for passive alternatives. That's where my mother came in as a consultant for the home plan. My mother loaded her Magic Couch into the trunk of her Nash Rambler convertible and headed into the field every weekday while most husbands were at work. She was always dressed to the nines in a black dress from Bullock's Wilshire with nylons, high-heeled shoes, gloves, and a hat. Leaving the Magic Couch in the Rambler, my mother made a grand entrance as she approached the prospect's door as if she was walking on air down the runway at the Tea Room.

My mother's sales process was like a kid's wooden jigsaw puzzle. In fact, she had my father create a puzzle for her with a jigsaw and let me paint the pieces: red, yellow, blue, and green. Her sales puzzle had only four pieces. The first piece, the red one, represented *Theory*. Theory includes knowledge about the product or service, the marketplace, and the competition. It can be called research, homework, or due diligence. It is crucial and fundamental to any selling process. My mother's red puzzle piece was the Stauffer Home Reducing Plan from her own perspective and personal experience with the Magic Couch. She learned about diet, exercise, and weight loss. She understood the magic of making women *feel* slimmer by diverting their attention away from pounds and inches and educating them about health, fitness, self-esteem, posture, and attitude.

My mother called her second puzzle piece, the yellow one, *Strategy*. That piece was made up of specific information about the prospect. Before visiting a woman's home, there might have been limited information about her. Most probably Mom only knew the woman's name, address, and phone number unless she was a personal referral or someone she had met socially or modeling. Most of the yellow puzzle piece came from her first few minutes with the prospect. After the woman opened the door and invited her to sit down, my mother always followed the same routine. Her signature line was: "Sometimes the best relationships begin with a simple introduction. My name is Marion Miller, and I am a Stauffer Consultant. Please call me 'Jinx' – my skating name. That would lead to the prospect asking for clarification about what my mother meant by 'skating name.' My mother would explain that, before getting married and having three kids, she was a fashion model and skated in Roller Derby. That usually caught the woman's attention. Those days Roller Derby was big on TV.

All of this time my mother was reading the woman's tells – verbal and non-verbal signals. And she was discretely scanning the inside of the house for hints about the woman. She looked for younger (perhaps thinner) photos of the woman. If she needed more time to appraise the woman and come up with a strategy, she would pull out her pink binder from her bag. She would tell the woman that she was going to share some photos with her and open the book and start paging through pictures of herself in a bathing suit poolside at the Beverly Hills Hotel or Ambassador or in an evening gown at the Coconut Grove. The photos had movie stars and celebrities – "glamorous, thin, beautiful" people. The woman usually engaged, and when my mother had mentally created her selling strategy, she would move on to the third puzzle piece just at the right time. She knew that timing is everything in magic.

SELLING

The third puzzle piece, the blue one, was called *Connect* and would be all about the woman and her feelings. She would ask the woman how she *felt* about her weight and appearance. My mother would never "fat shame" or infer that being slim was better than not. My mother shared that she gained a lot of weight during all three of her pregnancies and that it was tough to lose that weight after her babies were born. My mother had 100% of their attention. The magic question that my mother expected the woman to ask was: "How did you do it?" And that would lead to the fourth puzzle piece, the green one. With three of the four puzzle pieces in place, it was obvious where the fourth puzzle piece would go. The green piece was called *Sale* and was what most salespeople would call "the close." At this point, my mother would reach into her black bag and pull out her gold Mont Blanc fountain pen, notebook, a paper measuring tape, and a circular calorie calculator. With the woman watching, my mother would ask "Do you have a pair of scissors?" After being handed the scissors, my other would hold up the measuring tape and cut in into pieces. Then she would stare into the woman's eyes, smile, and tell her: "Let's not be concerned with inches!" She would do the same with the calorie calculator and then say: "Let's forget about calories." Watching the woman's reactions, she would ask: "Do you have a bathroom scale?" When the women admitted that she had a scale, my mother would say: "Let's forget about pounds and throw it out."

Having built up the anticipation of the demonstration, my mother would then ask: "Do you have time to try the magic couch, or do you want me to come back when your husband is home? Most of the time the woman would be anxious to try out the machine. My mother would then ask: "Are you serious about looking slimmer or just curious?" Usually, the woman would look little confused and then my mother would continue: "I am asking because I can only help a few women at a time and work with women who are committed to changing their lives. Magic Couches are selling like hotcakes, and I have to put some women on a waiting list."

My mom would then go out to the convertible and bring in her Magic Couch with her name "Jinx" on a brass nameplate. She would lay down on the machine for a few minutes before allowing the woman to experience it. Then, her magical words: "Like me (*you like me*), you want to look slim and feel slender. And, by now (*buy now*) you believe that you can rediscover your beauty and magic." Then Mom would ask "How do you want your name on your Magic Couch nameplate? Please spell it for me." (While she was thinking: "press hard, there are three copies.") Mom would tell them "...visualize yourself slim and slender," and when you feel that you have reached your goal you are going to buy a new dress and we are going to take some beautiful pictures of you. Imagine what you are going to look like on your Christmas card, birthday, daughter's wedding, or your reunion.

My mother shared stories about others to make them believe that they, too, could be slim and slender. Mom taught them the tricks of modeling like standing up straight and how to walk. My mother was the product, not the Magic Couch. My mother believed in herself and *the magic of selling*. Mom was the MAGIC!

Everyone lives by selling something.

–Robert Louis Stevenson

Principles

A bad salesman will automatically drop his price. Bad salesmen make me sick.

–Sam Stone (Danny DeVito)
Ruthless People (1966)

PRINCIPLES

Here are *thirteen principles* that will provide you with a basic understanding of how selling works. Memorize these thirteen principles, and you will never get yourself into a mess like Mickey Mouse did when he became the Sorcerer's Apprentice in *Fantasia.*

Walt Disney released *Fantasia* in 1940, and it has remained my favorite movie since I first saw it in the early 1950's.

The legend of the sorcerer's apprentice is a story over two thousand years old about an apprentice who was anxious to learn the sorcerer's magic tricks. He started trying to practice the magic tricks before he understood what he was doing. He tried using magic before he had learned how to control it.

In *Fantasia*, Mickey, as the Sorcerer's Apprentice, casts a spell on a broom to get it to carry water. Unfortunately, he could not get it to stop. Watch the video on YouTube, and you will get it. The soundtrack is hypnotic and there is a lesson to be learned (if not several). Don't let yourself get into a mess like Mickey.

1

You Are the Product

You are the product. You feel something. That's what sells. Not them. Not sex. They can't do what we do and they hate us for it.

—Don Draper (Jon Hamm)
Mad Men

You are the product. That is what you are selling, and that is what they are buying.

2

Buyers Are Liars

If you have the ability to convince somebody of something that you don't necessarily think is the case, it's a valuable asset. Not that I'm like a pathological liar, but we spend most of the day not fully being honest, you know?

—Leonardo DiCaprio

B uyers are liars is a term that car salespeople use because prospects come in with numbers that could only exist at Fantasyland Motors.

3

People Buy Emotionally

When dealing with people, remember that you are not dealing with creatures of logic, but with creatures of emotion.

—Dale Carnegie

We all think with our minds and buy with our emotions. Whether it's the red convertible or little black dress, it's all about how we *feel* and what we want because we want things that make us *feel* good.

4

Stories Sell

Truly, there is magic in fairy tales. For it takes but a simply uttered *"Once upon a time…"* to allure and spellbind an audience.

–Richelle E. Goodrich
Smile Away

My first book, *Rainmaking*, is subtitled: *Impacting the World Through the Power of Emotions and the Magic of Storytelling.* Storytelling has been the magic of selling since time began. If you are a good storyteller, you can be great salesperson.

5

One Size Does Not Fit All

One size does not fit all.

—Frank Zappa

Frank Zappa could not have said it better. Each of us has unique DNA and, individual life experiences, emotional triggers, and support network.

6

There Are Plenty of Fish

There are plenty of fish in the sea, so don't settle for a shark.

—Kalvin Valentine

There are plenty of prospects. You can maintain your dignity. Don't chase after anyone. Don't beg for business. And don't tolerate being disrespected.

7

Get Their Money

Only one thing counts in this world. Get them to sign on the line that is dotted.

—Blake (Alec Baldwin)
Glengarry Glen Ross (1992)

The day I started on Wall Street my manager told me: "Get their fucking money before someone else does!" Remember Leonardo DiCaprio (Jordan Belfort) in *The Wolf of Wall Street*: "I want you to go out there, and I want you to RAM Steve Madden stock down your client's throats. Till they fucking choke on it till they choke on it and buy 100,000 shares! That's what I want you to do. You be ferocious! You be relentless!"

8

You Can't Always Please 'Em

You can please some of the people all of the time, you can please some of the people all of the time, but you can't please all of the people all of the time.

—John Lydgate

Stop being a pleaser! Stop telling people that you want to "earn their business." You should have them lining up around the block to earn *your* business. Cal Worthington was not a used car salesman; he was a magician. When I was in high school, we lived near his Ford dealership. Passing by we would often see Cal filming television commercials with his "dog spot" which could be tiger, hippo, elephant, crocodile – or even an airplane. Cal had them lined up to BUY! Cal was the product – people wanted to buy a Ford from him because of his selling magic.

9

People Like to Feel Special

Sometimes we all need a unicorn to believe in. Sometimes we need a unicorn to believe in us.

—Claudia Bakker

All of us like to *feel* special. No matter how big our egos might be, we love to be stroked, rubbed, massaged and pumped up. That's human nature. How do we make other people feel special without seeming insincere or patronizing? We must learn to emphasize with them. Empathy is putting yourself in someone else's situation. Sympathy is feeling pity, sorrow, or compassion for someone else. The easiest way to understand the difference is that *empathy* means that you know how someone else feels but don't necessarily share their feelings.

10

It's All About the Experience

We're in the business of selling pleasure. We don't sell handbags or haute couture. We sell dreams.

—Alain Werthheimer

Think about *Alice in Wonderland.* Alice spots a White Rabbit in a waistcoat mumbling to himself that he is "late for a very important date." She follows him down a large rabbit hole, and the adventure begins. And what an adventure it is! Watch or read any version of the story, and you will be pulled into Alice's encounters with Tweedledum and Tweedledee, the Dodo (bird), the hookah-smoking Caterpillar, the Cheshire Cat, the Mad Hatter, the March Hare, the Dormouse, And there's the all of the playing card characters. Take them down the rabbit hole and give them the experience of their lives!

11

People Love to Buy

If someone likes you, they'll buy what you're selling, whether or not they need it.

—Gene Simmons

What are the main reasons people spend money? Once you understand what makes people buy things you will know how to sell anything. Here are the reasons people love to buy:

1. To feel important (luxury goods.
2. To feel happy (money can but it).
3. To feel attractive (plastic surgery).
4. To feel sexy (Victoria's Secret).
5. To feel safe (alarm system).
6. To feel comfortable (heated seats).
7. To feel special (recognition).
8. To feel excited (fast car).
9. To feel healthy (organic food).

12

People Need to Be Told

People want to be told what do so badly they'll listen to anyone.

—Don Draper (Jon Hamm)
Mad Men

An epic speech by Leonardo DiCaprio as Jordan Belfort in *The Wolf of Wall Street* (2013):

"So, you listen to me, and you listen well. Are you behind, on your credit card bills? Good. Pick up the phone and start dialing. Is your landlord ready to evict you? Good. Pick up the phone and start dialing. Does your girlfriend think you're a fucking loser? Good. Pick up the phone and start dialing! I want you to deal with your problems by becoming rich! All you have to do today… is pick up that phone and speak the words that I have taught you." Take control and tell them how the hog eats the cabbage!

13

Don't Oversell

You had me at hello.

—Dorothy Boyd (Rene Zellweger)
Jerry Maguire (1996)

Persistence is one thing; stupidity is another. Winners know when to quit — losers are desperate and keep chasing rainbows which have no pot of gold. Never run away but know when to back away from a deal gracefully. Create a demand for yourself and attract people to you. Then you can cherry-pick your best clients.

Humans are not ideally set up to understand logic; they are ideally set up to understand stories.

–Roger C. Schank

Tells

I used an extreme amount of eye motion, wriggling eyes and turning his whiskers and this seemed to be what hit the public – expressions.

–Otto Messmer on Felix's Personality

Verbal Tells

R eading verbal tells is a skill that takes some practice. Here are some examples:

1. Misdirection– when people make excuses that indicate that they mean the opposite of what they say.
2. Expressing Concerns – a defensive statement that indicates a fear of confronting objections head-on.
3. Loudness – loud and emphatic people are likely bluffing.
4. Uncertainty and Verbal Looseness – may be an indication that the person is bluffing.
5. Negative or Irritated Responses – more telling than affirmative responses and may be an indication that the person believes that he is dealing from a position of strength.

What are they saying? Listen carefully to every word and analyze any differences between what is being said and what is intended to be said.

Non–Verbal Tells

There is a *Glossary of Tells* at the back of *Rainmaking*. The way you listen, look, and move – and, according to how you react – are all non-verbal tells. The whole body speaks and reading these non-verbal tells is the most challenging part of selling. Non-verbal tells are an acid-test of a person's emotions. Some people are more emotionally transparent than others.

Non-verbal tells can indicate both positive and negative emotions. Examples of non-verbal tells are shaking hands, hugging, and other forms of touch. Eye contact is significant as are facial expressions and gestures. Face reading is a part of ancient Chinese medicine.

Facial expressions, "microexpressions," are vital to successful selling. Lasting only a moment they are the result of a conflicting voluntary and involuntary responses briefly displaying true emotions. Imagine playing poker with everybody wearing masks. Limited microexpressions.

If you're playing a poker game and you look around the table and can't tell who the sucker is, it's you.

—Paul Newman

Tricks

Making films is sort of like you're pulling off a magic trick. It's sort of like an illusion. It's not real but you want it to appear real, and all kinds of things go into that, from the clothes you're wearing to the make-up, to the light.

–Jeff Bridges

TRICKS

Whenever Felix the Cat got in a "fix" he would reach for his little magical bag of tricks.

Felix (the wonderful, wonderful) Cat has no advantage over you, here are *thirty-three tricks* from my personal signature magical bag of tricks.

In time you will create your own signature bag of tricks. The little bag that Felix carried could do almost anything. It could become anything that Felix needed.

In *The Magic of Selling*, like *The Twilight Zone*, "you're traveling through another dimension, a dimension not only of sight and sound but of mind. A journey into a wondrous land whose boundaries are full of imagination."

Every selling experience should be an exciting and magnificent adventure for everyone involved. As a *magician* that is your sole responsibility – to give your prospective clients the times of their lives. That will convert them into clients Submitted for your approval, here are your first thirty-three tricks. Abracadabra!

1

Make a Grand Entrance

We made our entrance into Paris. As for honors, we received all that we could possibly imagine, but they, though very well in their way, were not what touched me the most. What was really affecting was the tenderness and earnestness of the poor people, who, in spite of the taxes with which they were overwhelmed, were transported with joy at seeing us.

–Marie Antoinette

There is a reason that this is Trick #1. Every deal begins with an entrance – successful transactions start with a Grand Entrance which requires *power, grace, and style.*

2

Set the Tone

Define what your brand stands for, its core values and tone of voice, and then communicate consistently in those terms.

—Simon Mainwaring

Take control from the get-go by setting the tone of the negotiations. Formal or informal? Serious or humorous? How do you know? Within the first few nanoseconds, you will have read the tells and will know how to set the tone. Setting the tone requires constant changes to stay ahead of the conversation and bring it back on track if it begins to drift off course. Your intentional tells will enable you to control the deal. If you made a Grand Entrance, this is easy.

3

Establish Common Ground

Stories are common ground that allow people to connect, despite all our defenses and all our differences.

—Kate Forsyth

Identify any possible common ground as soon as possible and then tell a story to convince people that you share something. The story doesn't have to be true, but it must be believable. If it isn't credible, it could blow up in your face, and your deal will be dead. The best example is the *Mongolian Peasant Principle* created by Joseph Stalin's psychologist to choose between right and wrong – greed and integrity. Stalin's psychologist claimed, "everybody had a Mongolian peasant in his life." Your homework assignment is to Google "Mongolian Peasant Principle."

4

Be Larger Than Life

I have been uncompromising, peppery, intractable, monomaniacal, tactless, volatile, and oftentimes disagreeable… I suppose I'm larger than life.

—Bette Davis

Have you ever met anyone larger than life? I have. But, at the end of the day, why can't you appear 'larger than life' to the world?

5

Identify the Decision Maker

> A lot of people don't want to make their own decisions. They're too scared. It's much easier to be told what to do.
>
> —Marilyn Manson

Your reading of tells will reveal the decision makers. If you can't identify the decision makers, pay equal attention to all players at the risk of offending and alienating a decision maker for failure to recognize them. Decision makers can change during a deal. Someone may misrepresent that they are a decision maker. That is a common dealmaking trick and one that you can use. Defer the power of decision-making to a phantom person so that you have some wiggle-room.

6

Paint Pictures

I love to sell, to visualize something for someone and make them see it.

–Stanley Marcus

The most natural way to paint pictures is to tell stories. The images I create are designed to take people on an emotional journey down the Yellow Brick Road toward Oz. My favorite storytelling technique is "Dorothy's Front Door." You know the famous scene – when Dorothy walks out of her front door and for the first time the world sees Technicolor. I start out my stories in black and white and then, at the most dramatic moment, introduce Technicolor to my story. Make your stories, like *The Twilight Zone*, "a dimension not only of sight and sound but of mind." Paint pictures of colors, shapes, textures and add smells, and sounds.

7

Keep Them Guessing

He prizes ambiguity; he loves to keep you guessing.

—Lionel Shriver
We Need to Talk About Kevin

What is the most powerful effect of a story, book, or movie? Suspense is powerful. Don't tip your hat too early or go directly to cost. Often that is the only thing in which people have an interest. Don't put your all your cards on the table to quickly and never show your hand until there is no other choice. And always save your best play (deal) for last.

8

Distract Them

It consists admittedly in misleading the spectator's senses, in order to screen from detection certain details for which secrecy is required.

—Nevil Maskelyne

In magic circles, misdirection is the art of directing a person's attention away from where it is to where you want it to be. It is a form of deception which focuses an audience's attention on one thing to distract its attention from another. Misdirection is an essential skill of theatrical magic. Sleight of hand depends on the art of misdirection.

9

Be a Game Changer

In a world full of game players, the only way to set yourself apart is to be a game changer.

—Matshona Dhliyayo

I t's somewhat of a cliché but being a game changer is a big thing in dealmaking. Remember that YOU are the magic and that means that you are controlling the deal. To be a game changer, you must be on top of your game at all times. You can slow the game down, up the ante, and even take the deal off the table temporarily or permanently. The best way to be a game changer is to be the hero of the game. Start out by making it appear that there may not even be a viable deal to close. Put up obstacles, build walls, create road bumps, and then at the right moment, change the game.

10

Tell White Lies

A storyteller makes up things to help other people; a liar makes up things to help himself.

–Daniel Wallace
The Kings and Queens of Roam

Admit it. You've lied. You're not alone. Deception is everywhere around us. Many people lie regularly, and they're not just telling white lies. Some psychological experts don't differentiate between a white lie (telling grandma that the lime Jell-O was delicious) and a black lie (covering up an extramarital affair). White lies work (usually). People love compliments. They love anything that makes them feel good about themselves. Be careful what you say and how you say it. Telling someone: "you look great, you lost a lot of weight" could backfire with a response like: "Did I look fat before?"

11

Wear Black Socks

I never cheat, I practice
Gamesmanship —the art of winning
games without actually cheating.

–L.J. Smith
The Forbidden Game

My father played tennis for UCLA in the days when players dressed in white. When UCLA played USC, my father wore black socks. My father's gamesmanship threw off the players on the other side of the net. The magic of selling is about gamesmanship — the art of winning without cheating. Every client is unique, and every game is different. Because wearing black socks won't always work, gamesmanship must be impromptu. The game can change at any time, and you must be able to anticipate the changes and maintain control of the deal.

12

Climb Inside Their Skin

If you can learn a simple trick, Scout, you'll get along better with all kinds of folks. You never really understand a person until you consider things from his point of view, until you climb inside his skin and walk around in it.

–Atticus Finch
To Kill a Mockingbird –Harper Lee

There's a difference between being tolerant and embracing "diversity." And there's a difference between sympathy and empathy. You can climb inside someone's skin to try to figure out what it's like to be them. But it is an exceedingly rare trait to be able to understand how someone feels.

13

Cast a Spell

"Imperio!" Moody jerked his wand, and the spider rose onto two of his hind legs and went into what was unmistakably a tap dance. Everyone was laughing – except Moody. "Think it's funny, do you? he growled. "You'd like it, would you, if I did it to you? The laughter stopped almost instantly.

–J. K. Rowling
Harry Potter and the Goblet of Fire

C asting a spell is easier said than done. Call it getting them to drink the Kool-Aid or putting them under the ether. It takes focus and concentration to cast a spell. Make sure that you know how to end the spell. Remember Mickey's nightmare as the Sorcerer's Apprentice? Spells can be dangerous. Put them under the ether and keep them there as long as you can.

44

14

Sell Them Their Dreams

The excitement of dreams coming true is beyond the description of words.

–Lailah Gifty Akita

Peter Pan knew very well how to sell The Lost Boys their dreams. Most storytellers have that skill. Mark Twain knew how to sell dreams with his stories of Tom Sawyer and Huckleberry Finn. Sell them their dreams. Our dreams are priceless gifts that our hearts and minds keep. The excitement of dreams coming true is a powerful emotion that you can leverage to sell anything you want. Anyone can sell tangible goods and services to people, but it takes a wizard of selling to sell them their dreams. Remember that you have to know what *their* dreams are. You are not selling them your dreams – you are selling them theirs.

15

Pretend You're Done

Life's like a movie. Write your own ending. Keep believing, keep pretending.

—Jim Henson

Pretending to be finished is a trick demanding tremendous skill. It's like slowing a bike down as slow as you can without slowing it down so much that you start to fall over. You have to maintain some momentum. So how do you do this? You build momentum one step at a time like climbing a ladder. Then, once you have taken the deal to the first rung you, appraise the situation, you pretend to be finished, and people will relax and let down their defenses. Make sure you can get the deal rolling again. You don't want to lose a prospect on the operating table.

16

Mesmerize Them

The whole idea of being mesmerized and not in control of your own actions is a little spooky. I remember hearing about someone who'd gone to a magic act, and a person in the audience had become hypnotized by observing too closely by what the magician was doing on stage, and thought it was spooky to lose your consciousness that way.

–Chris Van Allsburg

Mesmerizing someone involves holding someone's attention to transfix them, dominate their thoughts, influence their actions. Franz Mesmer, a German physician, believed that there was a natural transference of energy between all animated and inanimate objects and called it mesmerism.

17

Give Them What They Want

I want ten chocolate chip cookies.
Medium chips. None too close to the
outside.

—Howard Hughes (Leonardo DiCaprio)
The Aviator (2004)

Who knows whether Howard Hughes was ever so specific about his chocolate chip cookies. But the line sounded great when Leonardo DiCaprio said it in *The Aviator.* Before you can sell them anything, you need to determine what they want and why. Remember you are going to give them what they want and not what you want. Otherwise, you will be running the risk of buyer's remorse.

18

Have Them Take Notes

He listens well who takes notes.

—Dante

This self-explanatory. Having them take notes gets them involved, Nothing more – nothing less. I use a Mont Blanc pen and am quick to offer it to them to them. My gesture is an act of trust. (Even though I once had one stolen under my eyes and captured on security video.)

19

Help Them With the Math

Mathematics is the music of reason.

—James Joseph Sylvester

When reviewing numbers in a deal, I always start out by saying: "Help me with the math."

20

Know Your Customer

The aim of marketing is to know and understand your customer so well the product or service fits him and sells itself.

—Peter Drucker

K nowing your customer has both legal implications and dealmaking advantages.

21

Always Be One Step Ahead

I'm always thinking one step ahead.
Like a carpenter that makes stairs.

—Andy Bernard

I admit that the Wayne Gretzky's "I skate where the puck is going not where it has been." has become an overused corporate cliché but nobody says it as well as the Great One.

22

Steer Into the Skid

A word of advice: Play along. The more you fight it, the worse it's gonna get. It's like when your car skids on ice, you steer into the skid.

—Ted Mosby (Josh Radnor)
How I Met Your Mother

H ead into the center of the storm. When you see a roadblock ahead, put your foot down harder because the other people might freeze like a deer in the headlights. Your immediate natural response may be to avoid issues and objections by steering away from the skid — always steer into the direction of the skid.

23

Know Your Facts

To be prepared is half the victory.

–Miguel de Cervantes

Knowledge is power - end of story.

24

Adjust Your Seat
and Be Humble

Civility is not a sign of weakness, and sincerity is always subject to proof.

—John F. Kennedy

You must pay close attention to this one. Many people are nervous or initially uncomfortable. So this is what you do. Before the meeting, adjust your chair at a lower height than the others. When the other people sit down, they will start out sitting higher than you and will feel somewhat superior to you. Sit down and be humble and civil. Remember what JFK said: "… sincerity is always subject to proof." As the meeting progresses you can slowly raise your seat height until you end up higher than them. Abracadabra!

25

Appear Vulnerable

To share your weakness is to make yourself vulnerable; to make yourself vulnerable is to show your strength.

—Criss Jami

Have you ever watched an animal pretend to be sick or dead? It's a trick that God gave animals to help them survive. You can do the same thing. Appear vulnerable. When you appear vulnerable, you give others a sense of false power just like you do when you adjust your seat. This trick can blow up if you don't execute it properly. Be careful not to overplay this one.

26

Have One More Thing

Oh, just one more thing…why would your wife have been out on the boat alone when she couldn't swim?

—Lieutenant Columbo (Peter Falk)
Columbo

This trick is epic and classic. And it is one that Peter Falk executed time and time again as Columbo. Having one more thing is an innocuous trick. It is simple but effective. Like Columbo, always have one more thing.

27

Demo Them

Any product that needs a manual to work is broken.

—Elon Musk

That's the most efficient way to sell a car? Give them a test drive. That's why Costco hands out food samples left and right. So you can see, smell, touch, and taste what they are selling. That's why the perfume counters at Nordstrom and Bloomingdale's have sample bottles out.

28

Make Them Think You're a Martyr

Being a martyr is highly recommended.

—Patricia Briggs
Dragon Bones

M ake them think that you are doing a great favor for them by giving them something extra or giving them a killer deal. That's all folks!

29

Let Them Sell You

We don't sell a car, we sell a dream. We are Italy's national team. There are many great soccer teams in our country, but there is only one Ferrari.

—Luca Cordero di Montezemolo

Create such a tremendous demand for yourself that they start trying to sell you before you have to sell them. Try it. It works!

30

Mimic Them

We ape, we mimic, we mock. We act.

–Sir Laurence Olivier

Aleister Crowley was a magician who believed he could control anyone with the power of his mind. One day in the 1920's Crowley was walking down a New York sidewalk with a friend who asked him for a demonstration of his skills as a magician. Crowley pointed to a man who was walking in front of them and began to mimic the man's walk and step. Then Crowley suddenly dropped down into a crouch, and the man he was imitating did the same. The man got up and brushed himself off and looked around for a banana peel or something that would have caused him to fall. The story is legendary in occult circles as proof of a concept they call "action at a distance." Mimic them!

31

Play Into Their Fears

The oldest and strongest emotion of
mankind is fear, and the oldest and
strongest kind of fear is the unknown.

–H. P. Lovercraft

Play into people's fears. More
prominent than the fear of the
unknown is FOMO (the *fear of
missing out.)*

32

Lose the Cheap Sales Talk

Our business is infested with idiots who try to impress by using pretentious jargon.

—David Ogilvy

When you sound like a salesman, people treat you like a salesman. Don't beg anyone for business. Lose these words and phrases NOW:

1. Earn your business.
2. Actually.
3. To tell you the truth.
4. To be honest with you.
5. Truthfully.
6. I always tell people...
7. I am not making any money on this...

33

Be a Wizard

In a way, we are magicians. We are alchemists, sorcerers, and wizards. We are a strange bunch. But there is great fun in being a wizard.

—Billy Joel

There are worse things in life than death. Have you ever spent an evening with an insurance salesman?

–Woody Allen

Secrets

And above all, watch with glimmering
eyes the whole world around you
because the greatest secrets are
always hidden in unlikely places.
Those who don't believe in magic will
never find it.

–Roald Dahl

SECRETS

Magician's Circles around the world have what they call **The Magician's Code** which means that they do not reveal their secrets. Here are my **Seven Secrets** that I am revealing to you knowing that I will not be shattering the illusion of Peter Pan but will be inspiring you to use the power of emotions and the magic of storytelling. You do not have to take The Magician's Oath swearing yourself to secrecy. Anyone can sell through deceptive means. The challenge, should you decide to accept it, is to sell ethically. There is no honor in being a cheat and a liar. Taking unfair advantage of people is not what *The Magic of Selling* is all about. *The Magic of Selling* is about making dreams come true. It is about selling magically. **Abracadabra!**

1

Timing

I'm such a profound believer that timing is everything; I would tattoo that on my arm.

—Drew Barrymore

Timing is everything in selling — that's why it's Secret #1. The magic is in being intuitive about when to put the pieces in the selling puzzle. Your timing must appear natural. Move too quickly, and you'll scare people away. Move too slowly, and you'll lose their attention. How do you perfect timing? You can't. No two deals are the same. You must be able to create your timeline as you progress through your magical selling process.

2

Patterns

Humans are pattern-seeking story-telling animals, and we are quite adept at telling stories about patterns, whether they exist or not.

—Michael Shermer

Selling magic requires you to be able to recognize patterns and take advantage of them. You must learn to predict trends and master the art of manipulating them to your advantage. Patterns come in all shapes and sizes. There are speech patterns and patterns of movement. There are time patterns and behavioral patterns. There are patterns of space and patterns of choices. You must be able to determine which ones carry the most weight.

3

Directing

Directing is very close to
choreography; you deal with
space, time, emotions, lighting,
making beautiful images.

—Benjamin Millepied

The choreography of selling is called
directing. Directing is how you
combine all of the elements of the
deal to command the attention of people
and take them where you want them to be.
Picture yourself as a puppeteer and your
clients being puppets. As cold and
straightforward as that might sound it's the
reality of selling. You have to be able to pull
strings and manipulate the puppets without
getting them all tangled in their lines.

4

Space

Sense of place is the sixth sense, an internal compass and map made by memory and special perception together.

—Rebecca Solnit

Quantum physics, quantum mechanics, or whatever you want to call it, it's all about space and relativity. Pilots are trained to have their heads on a swivel and always be aware of everything and everyone around them.

5

Numbers

When you have mastered numbers,
you will in fact no longer be reading
numbers, any more than you read
words when reading books. You will
be reading meanings.

—W. E. B. Du Bois

H ave your numbers and be able to
recite them drunk, drugged, or in
your sleep. Numbers can be
manipulated to your advantage when you
are selling. Just be sure of your numbers
before you use them.

6

Beliefs

We are, at almost every point of our day, immersed in cultural diversity: faces, clothes, smells, attitudes, values, traditions, behaviors, beliefs, rituals.

—Randa Abdel-Fattah

Both fundamental to, and paramount of, selling are the beliefs of all principals involved in every deal. You are not required to share the beliefs of others; nor are you expected to approve of them. You need to be able to put everyone's expectations in perspective. By understanding peoples' beliefs, you will be able to understand their motivations. And then you will be able to sell them.

7

Energy

If you want to find the secrets of the universe, think in terms of energy, frequency and vibration.

—Nikola Tesla

Energy, frequency, and vibration are catalysts that make deals happen. From where does the energy come? The strength comes from within. I believe that the power comes from God.

Now you're looking for the secret...
but you won't find it because of
course you're not really looking. You
don't really want to know. You want to
be fooled.

–Christopher Priest
The Prestige (2006)

Magic

I only hope that we never lose sight of
one thing – that it all started with a
mouse.

–Walt Disney

MAGIC

Magic is believing in yourself. J.M. Barrie, the creator of *Peter Pan,* said it all: "The moment you doubt whether you can fly, you cease for ever to be able to do it."

There are three keys to *The Magic of Selling*: (1) Believing in yourself; (2) Knowing *Why* you are selling; and (3) Being untouchable. Vishen Lakhiani calls it "unfuckwithable." (mindvalley.com). All three are equally important.

Peter Pan is all about believing. Peter is a free-spirited and mischievous young boy who can imagine things into existence. Peter believes he can fly and spends his never-ending childhood as the leader of the Lost Boys on the mythical island of Neverland. He has adventures with Indians, fairies, mermaids, and pirates. Peter Pan is a great salesman who is nonchalant and fearlessly cocky. And he claims greatness even when his claims might be unfounded. Peter Pan believes in magic and can emotionally transport others into his magical world because he is the magic. Believing in yourself in magic is the first key to your magic.

MAGIC

Why do you sell or why do you want to learn how to sell? If you need help figuring that out, I suggest that you *find your Why* by reading *Find Your Why* by Simon Sinek. Simon is a visionary who started a movement to inspire people to find their Why. Simon's book is an easy-to-follow guide that will start you on your journey of discovering the things that inspire you. Simon's concept of the Golden Circle influenced my book: *Rainmaking*. The second key to your magic is finding your Why.

The third key to your magic is to be *untouchable* — the state of mind in which no one can get you "off the market." Nothing in the past. Nothing in the present. Nothing in the future. Nothing can get you off the market. Whatever it takes to get keep you focused — white magic or even black.

Magic is what you make it. You can be manipulative and selfish. Or you can use your magic to help others realize their dreams. Let your conscience be your guide. Believe in yourself. Know why you sell. Be untouchable. That is the magic of selling. You are the magic. **Abracadabra!**

You never understood *why* we did this. The audience knows the truth… But if you can fool them even for a second, then you can make them wonder… it was a look on their faces.

–Robert Angier (Hugh Jackman)
The Prestige (2006)

Abracadabra

James Gordon Bennett:
Does it bother you that everything you are selling is fake?
P.T. Barnum:
Do these smiles seem fake?

—*The Greatest Showman* (2017)

ABRACADABRA

Aside from all of the quotes and between the lines of this book there is only one message. There is only one principle, only one trick, and only one secret. And that single is that you are the magic.

Somewhere along the way my first book, *Rainmaking*, became very idealistic and was published as a much different book than I had planned.

I planned this book, *The Magic of Selling*, and wrote it in two weeks. I wanted to keep it simple and easy to read. That's why it is 104 pages, has large fonts, and sixth-grade English.

The magic of selling is about connecting with other people by investing the time to feel what they are feeling. It's about listening to them and learning about their dreams. It's about empathizing with them and using stories to enchant them and make them believe that you can help them realize their dreams. Use stories to emotionally transport them through time and space. With the grace of God and the blood, sweat, and tears of my parents and grandparents, I grew up in a magical place

ABRACADABRA

at a magical time. My childhood could not have been more magical. I was born in 1947 when we were still pounding our chests from saving the Free World. We no longer needed ration stamps to buy gasoline or sugar. Cars were getting bigger, and so were waistlines. We were skipping down Main Street on the way to Fantasyland along with Mickey and Minnie and Donald and Daisy.

After surviving the Great Depression and WWII, my family was living the California Dream. My father was working at Douglas Aircraft and, my mother was selling The Magic Couch. I was watching *The Sorcerer's Apprentice* at the Million Dollar Theater and *Felix the Cat* cartoons on black and white television. I was surfing the beaches of my native sunny Southern California and didn't understand my parents telling me to eat my vegetables because kids were starving in Europe. I was under the magic of being a kid.
The magic stopped on November 22, 1963, like the music in Don McLean's *American Pie* ("Do you call what was revealed the day the music died? We started singing bye, bye, Miss American pie."). I have held

tight to that one brief shining moment of Camelot when we believed that we could change the world. The sixties started off with tours of the White House and ended with a *Magical Mystery Tour*.

Like JFK, I believe "To those whom much is given, much is expected." If you have God-given magical selling skills, you have a responsibility to do everything you can to impact the world positively. You can create great wealth through socially responsible investing and social entrepreneurship.

You have to believe that you are the magic. Magic comes from what's inside you. Remember what J. M. Barrie (the creator of Peter Pan) said: "The moment you doubt whether you can fly, you cease for ever to be able to do it." You can't weave a selling spell over someone if you don't believe in yourself and don't believe in the spell. God has given me the ability to sell magically, and I believe I have a responsibility to use those gifts to make a positive impact on the world. Every day I remind myself that I have a purpose. It may change often, but I stay on track to sell passionately and responsibly. Anyone, almost anyone, can sell by using lies and deception. The magic of selling is about selling with integrity.

What is magical selling? It's Walt Disney and his little mouse. It's Cal Worthington and his "dog" Spot. Selling combines magic and showmanship.

Steve Jobs was the perfect example of a magician and a showman. Jobs had that innate and perhaps inexplicable ability to sell anything to anyone.

Whether you are selling a product, a service, or your ideas, be a magician and a showman. Get people excited by telling them a story, getting them to visualize realizing their dreams and making them believe that you are the one that's going to help them make it happen. You can do it.

Magic is a big word – and a big world. There is white magic, black magic, and just magic. There is no accurate definition of "magic" because magic is what you make it. And magic has absolutely no value unless everyone believes in magic. Do you believe in magic? You must because you're reading *The Magic of Selling.*

We sure outfoxed them.

—Felix the Cat

PRESTIGE

I think people know Steve Jobs the showman. I think people know the guy who stood up and gave keynotes.
The magician.
The salesman.

—Ashton Kutcher

PRESTIGE

Great salesmen are magicians, sorcerers, alchemists, and wizards. They are illusionists, showmen, and entertainers who mesmerize their audiences and hold them spellbound. They tell stories that motivate and captivate and direct and misdirect the attention of others to close deals. They use "every trick in the book" to impress, enchant, and convince.

There is no official instruction manual for the magic of selling. This little book is a glance at the power that you will have by learning patterns of behavior, reading the tells, and mastering the rules, secrets, and tricks. You will then be empowered to persuade others without them knowing.

Just as I was getting ready to push the button to send my edited manuscript to be published, I came across a mashup of the movie *The Wizard of Oz* accompanied by Pink Floyd's *The Dark Side of the Moon*. *The Great Gig in the Sky* matches up with the tornado and my favorite part – when Dorothy opens the door to find Munchkin Land in Technicolor – is accompanied by the song *Money*.

PRESTIGE

Now I view *The Magic of Selling* as a virtual mashup of all my favorite magical movies and my passion for selling. And it may be a mashup of *caveat venditor* and *caveat emptor*. There's a line in *The Prestige* when Michael Caine (Cutter) tells Hugh Jackman (Angier): "You're a magician, not a wizard. You've got to get your hands dirty if you're going to achieve the impossible. Remember one thing: if you don't get their money someone else will. Take that to mean what you will. Watch the movie and you will learn a lot about what's real and what's not real. And you will discover that the difference is not always clear. Magic is only magic if you believe in magic. Do you believe in magic?

The Magic of Selling has one simple message: you are the magic! Dare to be great. Color outside the lines. Dance on the edge. Hold on tight to your dreams. Be willing to get your hands dirty. Wash your hands for lunch. Believe in yourself and in others. Positively impact the world. I wish you all the magic you can conjure up.

Abracadabra!

MY BOOKS

Rainmaking
Second Wind

CO-AUTHORED WITH HENRY PARK

C19 Economics
Fading Dreams and Rising Fears
Latino Investors Advisors & Entrepreneurs
Tossing the Masks

I'll see you on the dark side of the moon.

— *Brain Damage* – Pink Floyd
Roger Waters (1979)

www.ingramcontent.com/pod-product-compliance
Lightning Source LLC
Chambersburg PA
CBHW060629210326
41520CB00010B/1535